The Complete Guide to Pressure And Water Bath Canning

Simple, Safe, Step by Step Instructions To Master Home Canning Recipes | Ball Canning Cookbook Practical Guide

© Copyright 2020 Diane Devero - All rights reserved.

The content contained within this book may not be reproduced, duplicated or transmitted without direct written permission from the author or the publisher.

Under no circumstances will any blame or legal responsibility be held against the publisher, or author, for any damages, reparation, or monetary loss due to the information contained within this book. Either directly or indirectly. You are responsible for your own choices, actions, and results.

Legal Notice:

This book is copyright protected. This book is only for personal use. You cannot amend, distribute, sell, use, quote or paraphrase any part, or the content within this book, without the consent of the author or publisher.

Content

Chapter 1 : All You Need To Know About Canning And Preserving

Chapter 2: Definition of Terms Used in Canning

Chapter 3 : Fruit Canning Recipes

Chapter 4 : Vegetables Canning Recipes

Chapter 5 : Meat Canning Recipes

Chapter 6 : Notes

Chapter 1: All You Need To Know About Canning And Preserving

Important

Read Very carefully the following fundamental rules for canning and preserving. A thorough knowledge of these points will eliminate numerous difficulties that might otherwise be experienced.

Preserve fruit as soon as possible after picking.

Avoid using any fruit that is overripe or decayed.

Most fruits are better slightly under ripe than too ripe.

Can vegetables while they are fresh.

Use the method of canning best adapted to the kind of fruit you wish to can.

Always sterilize Jars and Caps by boiling them for 20 to 30 mins.

Never try to wipe the overflowing juice off the rubber or the Jar before the Jar is sealed.

To open Jars, pour fairly hot water on the top of the Jar, and the Cap can be easily unscrewed.

It is important that the Jars be stored in a cool, dry place.

There are certain essentials for the successful canning of fruits or vegetables. These include:

Good clean fresh materials, perfect containers, including good rubbers, heating for sufficient time to insure preservation, and air tight sealing. The necessities must be secured in any method of canning. The details of procedure may differ yet all have as their object the prevention of spoilage.

Sugarless Canning

All fruits may be canned fruitfully without the use of sugar by only adding hot water instead of hot syrup. If the fruit is perfectly sterilized and sealed, it will keep; so the addition of sugar is only a matter of taste. In canning fruit without sugar, *can the product the day it is picked*. Prepare the fruit, pack carefully in hot glass jars until jars are full. Fill the jar to overflowing with boiling water, put on rubber and top, screwing down to just touch the rubber. Proceed with the Cold Pack Method of cooking. If fruits shrink, do not open jar to fill-up. The space left is a sterilized vacuum and will not harm the contents. Sugarless canned fruit may be used for *pies, jellies, desserts* and *salads*, or as *table fruit* by sweetening when serving.

Directions for Making Syrup

To make a syrup appropriate for basic canning, take a pound of sugar to two and one-half large cups of water. This can be varied to suit the taste. If a sweeter syrup is preferred, more sugar may be added. The guidelines in this book sometimes call for a heavy syrup. Make this syrup by boiling together three pounds of granulated sugar and a quart of water. This makes one and a fourth pints syrup. This should be boiled until it shows signs of threading. At this point it should be put in the jar at once, for should it boil longer it will candy in the bottom of the jars. If more syrup is needed, use more sugar and water, in the same proportion as above. The syrup should always be boiling when poured into the jar.

Food preservation is the process of treating and handling food in such a way as to stop or greatly slow down spoilage and prevent foodborne illness while maintaining nutritional value, texture and flavor. Among the oldest methods of preservation are drying, refrigeration, and fermentation.

Canning is a modern method to preserve food, where we put food in jars at high temperatures for a long period. When you heat up the filled, sealed jars, it causes the foods to expand and give up steam, pushing air out of the jars. When cooled, it forms a vacuum seal on the jar.

Things that can affect canning and shelf life are the sugar content and acidity, it is best to follow a canning recipe when first starting to help decide which method is suited towards the food you will be canning.

Canning Benefits

Food preservation can result in several advantages, some of which are substantial.

It prevents the food from being spoiled by the action of enzymes and microorganisms, increases the safe storage period of foodstuffs, ensures round the year availability of seasonal foods, preservation in some cases produces a different form of the products which are of great importance in various cuisines (raisins, squash and wines made from grapes), and most importantly, increases the variety of foods, some with enhanced sensory properties and nutritional attributes.

Chapter 2: Definition of Terms Used in Canning

BLANCH.

Blanching means parboiling. Vegetables are put into boiling water for from one to fifteen minutes to soften, clean and sterilize them.

COLD DIP.

To drop the product quickly into cold water immediately after blanching.

PROCESSING.

This means cooking for a certain length of time.

HOT-WATER BATH.

An usual wash boiler, home canner, in which Jars can be sited to be sterilized. It must have a false bottom which may be made of wooden slats, or a tray with lifting handles to keep the Jars from setting directly on the bottom of the boiler, and should have a tight-fitting cover.

WATER-SEAL OUTFIT.

This apparatus contains an inner seal or jacket and a cover that passes into the seal and between the outer and inner jackets. This outfit is good for canning meats, for a higher pressure can be kept up than in the hot-water bath.

STEAM PRESSURE COOKERS.

These are kettles in which a fixed pressure of steam may be kept up. They are equipped with steam-gauge, pet-cock, safety-valve, etc.

Chapter 3: Fruit Canning

Pluots Recipe

- Get 2 pounds of Pluots.

- Wash and peel your Pluots.

- To peel the Pluots you will have to dip them in boiling water for 30 seconds to 2 minutes, depending on how ripe your Pluots are. Remove them from the boiling water and put the Pluots in a large bowl of cold water and ice for 3 to 5 minutes until they cool down. The skins now can easily slide off.

- Cut the Pluots as you prefer in half or to thin slices.

- To prepare the sweetener, in a large pot, you will add 8 cups of water or any fruit juice and 4 cups of sugar, stir the mixture for 10 to 15 minutes at a medium temperature.

- Fill the jars with the peeled and sliced Pluots leaving ½ headspace.

- Pour the sweetener over the Pluots in the jars and make sure to release any trapped air bubble you can using a knife or a spoon.

- Wipe any spills, seal and tighten the ring around the jars.

- Put the jars in a canner and cover them with water (1 to 2 inches above the jars) boil them for 20 minutes.

- Leave the jars to cool for 1 to 2 hours.

- And your Pluots are ready to be stored.

Plums Recipe

- [ ] Get 2 pounds of Plums.

- [ ] Wash and peel your Plums.

- [ ] To peel the Plums you will have to dip them in boiling water for 30 seconds to 2 minutes, depending on how ripe your Plums are. Remove them from the boiling water and put the Plums in a large bowl of cold water and ice for 3 to 5 minutes until they cool down. The skins now can easily slide off.

- [ ] Cut the Plums as you prefer in half or to thin slices.

- [ ] To prepare the sweetener, in a large pot, you will add 8 cups of water or any fruit juice and 4 cups of sugar, stir the mixture for 10 to 15 minutes at a medium temperature.

- [ ] Fill the jars with the peeled and sliced Plums leaving ½ headspace.

- [ ] Pour the sweetener over the Plums in the jars and make sure to release any trapped air bubble you can using a knife or a spoon.

- [ ] Wipe any spills, seal and tighten the ring around the jars.

- [ ] Put the jars in a canner and cover them with water (1 to 2 inches above the jars) boil them for 20 minutes.

- [ ] Leave the jars to cool for 1 to 2 hours.

- [ ] And your Plums are ready to be stored.

Nectarine Recipe

- Get 2 pounds of Nectarines.

- Wash and peel your Nectarines.

- To peel the Nectarines you will have to dip them in boiling water for 30 seconds to 2 minutes, depending on how ripe your Nectarines are. Remove them from the boiling water and put the Nectarines in a large bowl of cold water and ice for 3 to 5 minutes until they cool down. The skins now can easily slide off.

- Cut the Nectarines as you prefer in half or to thin slices.

- To prepare the sweetener, in a large pot, you will add 8 cups of water or any fruit juice and 4 cups of sugar, stir the mixture for 10 to 15 minutes at a medium temperature.

- Fill the jars with the peeled and sliced Nectarines leaving ½ headspace.

- Pour the sweetener over the Nectarines in the jars and make sure to release any trapped air bubble you can using a knife or a spoon.

- Wipe any spills, seal and tighten the ring around the jars.

- Put the jars in a canner and cover them with water (1 to 2 inches above the jars) boil them for 20 minutes.

- Leave the jars to cool for 1 to 2 hours.

- And your Nectarines are ready to be stored.

Strawberries Recipe

- [ ] Get 4 cups of sweet Strawberries.
- [ ] Wash and remove any mushy Strawberries.
- [ ] Grind or finely chop the Strawberries.
- [ ] In a pot, add your ground or chopped Strawberries with 2 cups of sugar and let the mixture boil at a medium temperature for 10 to 15 minutes.
- [ ] It is necessary to skim any excessive foam at the end of the boiling process.
- [ ] Fill the jars with the Strawberry mixture in the pot leaving ½ headspace.
- [ ] Wipe any spills, seal and tighten the ring around the jars.
- [ ] Put the jars in a canner and cover them with water (1 to 2 inches above the jars) boil them for 20 minutes.
- [ ] Leave the jars to cool for 1 to 2 hours.
- [ ] And your Strawberry jam is ready to be stored.

Watermelon Recipe

- [ ] Get a sweet and ripe watermelon.

- [ ] Wash, cut and dice the watermelon make sure to remove most of the seeds.

- [ ] Puree the watermelon in a blender or food processor until smooth.

- [ ] Since watermelons are not acidic, add the lemon juice to the pot. It is key to the safety of this recipe!

- [ ] In a pot, dump your watermelon puree with 2 cups of sugar and let the mixture boil at a medium temperature for 10 to 15 minutes.

- [ ] It is necessary to skim any excessive foam at the end of the boiling process.

- [ ] Fill the jars with the watermelon mixture in the pot leaving ½ headspace.

- [ ] Wipe any spills, seal and tighten the ring around the jars.

- [ ] Put the jars in a canner and cover them with water (1 to 2 inches above the jars) boil them for 20 minutes.

- [ ] Leave the jars to cool for 1 to 2 hours.

- [ ] And your watermelon jelly is ready to be stored.

Peaches Recipe

- [ ] Get 2 pounds of Peaches.

- [ ] Wash and peel your Peaches.

- [ ] To peel the Peaches you will have to dip them in boiling water for 30 seconds to 2 minutes, depending on how ripe your peaches are. Remove them from the boiling water and put the Peaches in a large bowl of cold water and ice for 3 to 5 minutes until they cool down. The skins now can easily slide off.

- [ ] Cut the Peaches as you prefer in half or to thin slices.

- [ ] Get 2 pounds of Peaches.

- [ ] Wash and peel your Peaches.

- [ ] To peel the Peaches you will have to dip them in boiling water for 30 seconds to 2 minutes, depending on how ripe your peaches are. Remove them from the boiling water and put the Peaches in a large bowl of cold water and ice for 3 to 5 minutes until they cool down. The skins now can easily slide off.

- [ ] Cut the Peaches as you prefer in half or to thin slices.

Pineapple Recipe

- [ ] Get a pineapple.
- [ ] Wash and peel your pineapple.
- [ ] Cut your pineapple to medium slices, or to small cubes.
- [ ] To prepare the sweetener, in a pot, you will add 2 cups of water or any fruit juice on a 1/2 cup of sugar. Stir the mixture at a medium temperature for 5 to 10 minutes.
- [ ] Fill the jars with the sliced pineapple leaving ½ headspace.
- [ ] Pour the sweetener over the pineapple in the jar and make sure to release any trapped air bubbles inside the jars.
- [ ] Wipe any spills, seal and tighten the ring around the jars.
- [ ] Put the jars in a canner and cover them with water (1 to 2 inches above the jars) boil them for 20 minutes.
- [ ] Leave the jars to cool for 1 to 2 hours.
- [ ] And your Pineapple is ready to be stored.

Citrus Recipe

- [ ] Get 2 pounds of your citrus fruit.
- [ ] Wash and peel your fruit, remove any remaining white spongy portion of the rind.
- [ ] Pull or slice the oranges or lemons as you prefer in half or segments.
- [ ] To prepare the sweetener, in a pot you will add 5 cups of water or orange juice on a 2 cup of sugar. Stir the mixture at a medium temperature for 5 to 10 minutes.
- [ ] Fill the jars with the sliced prepared citrus fruit leaving ½ headspace.
- [ ] Pour the sweetener over the citrus fruits in the jar and make sure to release any trapped air bubbles inside the jars.
- [ ] Wipe any spills, seal and tighten the ring around the jars.
- [ ] Put the jars in a canner and cover them with water (1 to 2 inches above the jars) boil them for 20 minutes.
- [ ] Leave the jars to cool for 1 to 2 hours.
- [ ] And your Citrus fruits are ready to be stored.

Sweet Cherries Recipe

- Get 4 cups of sweet cherries.

- Wash and remove all cherry pits.

- The grind of finely chop the cherries.

- In a pot, add your ground or chopped cherries with 2 cups of sugar and let the mixture boil at a medium temperature for 10 to 15 minutes.

- It is necessary to skim any excessive foam at the end of the boiling process.

- Fill the jars with the Cherry mixture in the pot leaving ½ headspace.

- Wipe any spills, seal and tighten the ring around the jars.

- Put the jars in a canner and cover them with water (1 to 2 inches above the jars) boil them for 20 minutes.

- Leave the jars to cool for 1 to 2 hours.

- And your cherry jam is ready to be stored.

Blackberries Recipe

- [ ] Get 6 of fresh or frozen blackberries.

- [ ] Wash and sort the berries, removing any leaves or mushy berries.

- [ ] To crush the berries, you can use a potato masher and crush each one layer at a time of berries or you can easily use slice mode on your food processor for quicker results.

- [ ] In a big pot, add 2 tablespoons of lemon juice on the crushed blueberries and a medium temperature stir the mixture until soft (about 5 to 10 minutes).

- [ ] Strain the hot berries through a colander; let them drain until they are cool enough. If you want a more clarified syrup, you can double strain the blackberries in a cheesecloth.

- [ ] To prepare the sweetener, in a pot, you will add 3 cups of water or any fruit juice on a ½ cup of sugar. Stir the mixture at a medium temperature for 5 to 10 minutes. If you want a syrup with whole fruit pieces, you can easily add a cup of blueberries to the sweetener.

- [ ] Mix the sweetener with the premade syrup.

- [ ] Fill the jars with the strained blueberry syrup leaving ½ headspace.

- [ ] Wipe any spills, seal and tighten the ring around the jars.

- [ ] Put the jars in a canner and cover them with water (1 to 2 inches above the jars) boil them for 20 minutes.

- [ ] Leave the jars to cool for 1 to 2 hours.

- [ ] And your Blackberry syrup is ready to be stored.

Apricots Recipe

- [ ] Get 2 pounds of apricots.

- [ ] Wash and peel your apricots.

- [ ] To peel the apricots you will have to dip them in boiling water for 30 seconds to 2 minutes, depending on how ripe your apricots are. Remove them from the boiling water and put the apricots in a large bowl of cold water and ice for 3 to 5 minutes until they cool down. The skins now can easily slide off.

- [ ] Cut the apricots as you prefer in half or to thin slices.

- [ ] To prepare the sweetener, in a large pot, you will add 8 cups of water or any fruit juice and 4 cups of sugar, stir the mixture for 10 to 15 minutes at a medium temperature.

- [ ] Fill the jars with the peeled and sliced apricots leaving ½ headspace.

- [ ] Pour the sweetener over the apricots in the jars and make sure to release any trapped air bubble you can using a knife or a spoon.

- [ ] Wipe any spills, seal and tighten the ring around the jars.

- [ ] Put the jars in a canner and cover them with water (1 to 2 inches above the jars) boil them for 20 minutes.

- [ ] Leave the jars to cool for 1 to 2 hours.

- [ ] And your apricots are ready to be stored.

Apples Recipe

- [ ] Get 4 pounds apples.
- [ ] Wash the apples, peel and remove the seeds or any hard part around the seeds.
- [ ] Cut the apples in thin slices.
- [ ] In a large pot, place the apple slices, add 1 gallon of boiling water or apple juice, and at a medium temperature blanch the apples for 5 minutes.
- [ ] Drain the apples and make sure you cover the apples while they are being drained so that they keep their moist texture.
- [ ] Do not forget to save the liquid where the apples were blanched you will need it later.
- [ ] Fill the jars with the blanched apple slices leaving ½ headspace.
- [ ] Pour the liquid where the apples where blanched over the apples in the jars.
- [ ] Wipe any spills, seal and tighten the ring around the jars.
- [ ] Put the jars in a canner, cover them with water (1 to 2 inches above the jars), and boil them for 20 minutes.
- [ ] Leave the jars to cool for 1 to 2 hours.
- [ ] And your apples are ready to be stored.

Chapter 4 : Canning Vegetables

Sweet Potatoes Recipe

- [ ] Get 13 pounds of well-shaped sweet potatoes.
- [ ] Wash the sweet potatoes.
- [ ] Boil the sweet potatoes until they are partially soft wait until they cool down then peel them
- [ ] Cut the sweet potatoes to little small cubes.
- [ ] Fill the jars with the Sweet Potatoes leaving ½ headspace.
- [ ] Pour boiling water in the jars, and make sure to release any trapped air bubbles in the jar.
- [ ] Wipe any spills, seal and tighten the ring around the jars.
- [ ] Put the jars in a canner and cover them with water (1 to 2 inches above the jars) boil them for 20 minutes.
- [ ] Leave the jars to cool for 1 to 2 hours.
- [ ] And your Sweet Potatoes are ready to be stored.

Onions Recipe

- [ ] Get 2 Pounds of Onions.

- [ ] Wash and peel the onions.

- [ ] Cut the Onions to thin slices, the thinner the slice the quicker it will be pickled, the thicker the slice the crunchier it is.

- [ ] In a small pot, mix apple cider vinegar with distilled vinegar.

- [ ] Fill the jars with the sliced onions.

- [ ] Pour the Vinegar mixture on the sliced onions in the jars.

- [ ] You can add a teaspoon of honey to break the vinegary taste of the onions.

- [ ] Wipe any spills, seal and tighten the ring around the jars.

- [ ] And your Sweet Potatoes are ready to be stored

Sweet Corn Recipe

- [ ] Get 3 to 4 fresh sweet corn.
- [ ] Husk your corn and pick off all the silk. You can use a vegetable brush for faster results.
- [ ] Cut or scrape the kernels from the cobs.
- [ ] In a pot, dump the cut kernels and add 1 cup of water in each quart of corn. Heat the corn to boiling and simmer 5 minutes.
- [ ] Fill the jars with the kernels leaving ½ headspace.
- [ ] Pour the liquid where the kernels were boiled over the corn in the jar and make sure to release any trapped air bubbles inside the jars.
- [ ] Wipe any spills, seal and tighten the ring around the jars.
- [ ] Process the jars in a pressure canner and cover them with water (1 to 2 inches above the jars) boil them for 55 minutes.
- [ ] Leave the jars to cool for 1 to 2 hours.
- [ ] And your Sweet Corn is ready to be stored.

Beans Recipe

- ❏ Ge about 14 pounds of beans.
- ❏ Wash the green or beans.
- ❏ Trim the ends and cut the beans into smaller pieces you can cut them in half.
- ❏ Fill the jars with the cut beans leaving ½ headspace.
- ❏ Pour boiling water into over the beans in the jars.
- ❏ Wipe any spills, seal and tighten the ring around the jars.
- ❏ Put the jars in a canner and cover them with water (1 to 2 inches above the jars) boil them for 30 to 40 minutes.
- ❏ Leave the jars to cool for 1 to 2 hours.
- ❏ And your beans are ready to be stored.

Asparagus Recipe

- [ ] Get the amount you want to can of asparagus.
- [ ] Wash the asparagus and trim off the tough scales.
- [ ] Cut the spears to fit your jars, leaving room for 1 inch of headspace. If you want, you can cut it to small pieces.
- [ ] Fill the jars with the cut asparagus leaving ½ headspace.
- [ ] Add 1 tablespoon of salt.
- [ ] Pour boiling water into over the asparagus in the jars.
- [ ] Wipe any spills, seal and tighten the ring around the jars.
- [ ] Put the jars in a canner and cover them with water (1 to 2 inches above the jars) boil them for 40 to 1 hour.
- [ ] Leave the jars to cool for 1 to 2 hours.
- [ ] And your asparagus is ready to be stored.

Carrots Recipe

- ☐ Get the amount you want to can of carrots.
- ☐ Wash and trim off the ends of the carrots.
- ☐ Cut the carrots to small slices. If you want, you can cut it to small pieces.
- ☐ Fill the jars with the cut carrots leaving ½ headspace.
- ☐ Add 1 tablespoon of salt.
- ☐ Pour boiling water into over the carrots in the jars.
- ☐ Wipe any spills, seal and tighten the ring around the jars.
- ☐ Put the jars in a canner and cover them with water (1 to 2 inches above the jars) boil them for 40 to 1 hour.
- ☐ Leave the jars to cool for 1 to 2 hours.
- ☐ And your carrots are ready to be stored.

Turnip Recipe

- [ ] Get the amount you want to can of Turnip.
- [ ] Wash and trim off the ends of the Turnip.
- [ ] Cut the Turnips to medium slices. If you want, you can cut it to small pieces.
- [ ] Fill the jars with the cut Turnip leaving ½ headspace.
- [ ] Add 1 tablespoon of salt.
- [ ] Pour boiling water into over the Turnip in the jars.
- [ ] Wipe any spills, seal and tighten the ring around the jars.
- [ ] Put the jars in a canner and cover them with water (1 to 2 inches above the jars) boil them for 40 to 1 hour.
- [ ] Leave the jars to cool for 1 to 2 hours.
- [ ] And your Turnip is ready to be stored.

Hot Pepper Recipe

- ❏ Get 9 pounds of hot pepper.
- ❏ Wash and remove stems, cores, and seeds of the pepper.
- ❏ Cut the pepper in half.
- ❏ Boil the peppers in water for 3 to 5 minutes then drain it.
- ❏ Fill the jars with the boiled drained pepper leaving ½ headspace.
- ❏ Add 1 tablespoon of salt.
- ❏ Pour the boiling water into over the Turnip in the jars.
- ❏ Wipe any spills, seal and tighten the ring around the jars.
- ❏ Put the jars in a canner and cover them with water (1 to 2 inches above the jars) boil them for 40 to 1 hour.
- ❏ Leave the jars to cool for 1 to 2 hours.
- ❏ And your Hot peppers are ready to be stored.

Tomato Sauce Recipe

- Get about 40 lbs. of tomatoes.

- Clean and peel the tomatoes.

- To peel the tomatoes you will have to dip them in boiling water for 30 seconds to 2 minutes, depending on how ripe your tomatoes are. Remove them from the boiling water and put the tomatoes in a large bowl of cold water and ice for 3 to 5 minutes until they cool down. The skins now can easily slide off.

- Cut the tomatoes in quarters and remove the tough part around the stem, any bruised or soft parts, seeds and excess water.

- In a pot, put half quantity of the tomatoes crush them with a spoon, you don't need to add water the tomatoes have enough juice, at a medium temperature keep stirring the tomatoes to prevent any burning, when boiling add the other half of the tomatoes this time you don't need to crush them.

- Before filling the jars with the tomatoes, add 5 tablespoons of lemon juice to retain the color, flavor and to reduce odd spoilage.

- Fill the jars with the tomatoes in the pot leaving ½ headspace.

- Wipe any spills, seal and tighten the ring around the jars.

- Put the jars in a canner and cover them with water (1 to 2 inches above the jars) boil them for 20 minutes.

- Leave the jars to cool for 1 to 2 hours.

- And your tomatoes are ready to be stored.

Tomato Paste Recipe

- [ ] Get 8 quarts Tomatoes Roma type.

- [ ] Clean and peel the tomatoes.

- [ ] To peel the tomatoes you will have to dip them in boiling water for 30 seconds to 2 minutes, depending on how ripe your tomatoes are. Remove them from the boiling water and put the tomatoes in a large bowl of cold water and ice for 3 to 5 minutes until they cool down. The skins now can easily slide off.

- [ ] Cut the tomatoes in quarters and remove the tough part around the stem, any bruised or soft parts, seeds and excess water.

- [ ] Blend your tomatoes until it is smooth.

- [ ] In a big pot, combine the tomatoes after blending, ½ cup of sweet red pepper, 3 bay leaves, and 2 teaspoons of salt, at a low temperature leave the tomatoes for 45 minutes to 1 hour until the paste get thicken while stirring every 15 minutes.

- [ ] Before filling the jars with the tomatoes, add 5 tablespoons of lemon juice to retain the color, flavor and to reduce odd spoilage.

- [ ] Fill the jars with the tomatoes in the pot leaving ½ headspace.

- [ ] Wipe any spills, seal and tighten the ring around the jars.

- [ ] Put the jars in a canner and cover them with water (1 to 2 inches above the jars) boil them for 20 minutes.

- [ ] Leave the jars to cool for 1 to 2 hours.

- [ ] And your tomatoes are ready to be stored.

Spiced Green Tomato Recipe

- [ ] Get 6 pounds small completely green tomatoes.

- [ ] Clean and peel the tomatoes.

- [ ] To peel the tomatoes you will have to dip them in boiling water for 30 seconds to 2 minutes, depending on how ripe your tomatoes are. Remove them from the boiling water and put the tomatoes in a large bowl of cold water and ice for 3 to 5 minutes until they cool down. The skins now can easily slide off.

- [ ] In a pot combine the peeled tomatoes, 8 cups of sugar, 1 pint of cider vinegar, 1 tablespoon of cloves and 1 tablespoon of allspice, at medium temperature boil them for 15 minutes. DO NOT STIR IT UNLESS IT WAS NECESSARY.

- [ ] Strain the tomatoes and save the packing solution you will need it for later.

- [ ] Fill the jars with the tomatoes but do not pack it too tightly leaving ½ headspace.

- [ ] Pour the liquid where the tomatoes were boiled on the tomatoes and make sure to release any trapped air bubbles in the jar.

- [ ] Wipe any spills, seal and tighten the ring around the jars.

- [ ] Put the jars in a canner and cover them with water (1 to 2 inches above the jars) boil them for 20 minutes.

- [ ] Leave the jars to cool for 1 to 2 hours.

- [ ] And your Spiced Green Tomatoes are ready to be stored.

Pickled Tomato Recipe

- [ ] Get 10 lbs. of green tomatoes and 2 onions.
- [ ] Wash the tomatoes and onions.
- [ ] Slice the green tomatoes and onions to medium slices.
- [ ] In a bowl place tomatoes and onions, then add ¼ cup of salt and let them stand for 6 hours
- [ ] Drain the tomatoes and onions from the liquid they will release.
- [ ] In a pot, combine 3 cups of white vinegar, 1 tablespoon of brown sugar, allspice, celery seed, cloves, and mustard seed.
- [ ] Add the tomatoes and onions to the mixture in the pot, at a low temperature simmer it for 20 to 30 minutes while stirring to prevent burning.
- [ ] Fill the jars with the tomatoes and onions, but do not pack it too tightly leaving ½ headspace
- [ ] Pour the liquid where the tomatoes and onions were simmered in the jars, and make sure to release any trapped air bubbles in the jar.
- [ ] Wipe any spills, seal and tighten the ring around the jars.
- [ ] Put the jars in a canner and cover them with water (1 to 2 inches above the jars) boil them for 20 minutes.
- [ ] Leave the jars to cool for 1 to 2 hours.
- [ ] And your pickled green tomatoes are ready to be stored.

Chapter 5 : Canning Meat

Beef Recipe

- [ ] Get your beef
- [ ] Wash and remove any excess fat, silver skin, or gristle.
- [ ] Cut your meat to medium sliced cube.
- [ ] Fill your jars with cubed meat leaving about 1 to 2-inch headspace.
- [ ] Add 1-teaspoon salt to each jar.
- [ ] Pour boiling water into each jar.
- [ ] Wipe any spills, seal and tighten the ring around the jars.
- [ ] Add lids and rings to jars, tightening just to finger-tight. No need to wrench the lids on with all your strength.
- [ ] Put your jars into the pressure canner and set on a rack inside the canner.
- [ ] Turn the heat back on and allow the pressure to build-up.
- [ ] Once the steam is pouring out through the valve, set a timer and allow it to continue venting for 10 minutes.
- [ ] Leave the jars to cool for 1 to 2 hours.
- [ ] And your beef ready to be stored.

Chicken Recipe

- ☐ Get your chicken.
- ☐ Wash; remove any fats, silver skin, or bones.
- ☐ Cut the chicken into cubes and make sure that the cubes will fit into your jars.
- ☐ Boil or bake to steam the chicken until it is 2/3 done.
- ☐ Fill the jars with the chicken cubes. Add salt if desired.
- ☐ Pour hot boiling water on the chicken in the jars.
- ☐ Wipe any spills, seal and tighten the ring around the jars.
- ☐ Add lids and rings to jars, tightening just to finger-tight. No need to wrench the lids on with all your strength.
- ☐ Put your jars into the pressure canner and set on a rack inside the canner.
- ☐ Turn the heat back on and allow the pressure to build-up.
- ☐ Once the steam is pouring out through the valve, set a timer and allow it to continue venting for 10 minutes.
- ☐ Leave the jars to cool for 1 to 2 hours.
- ☐ And your chicken ready to be stored.

Fish Recipe

- ☐ Get your fresh fish (Salmon, Tuna...)
- ☐ Wash and get rid of the viscera, the head and tale.
- ☐ Cut the fish to steaks or fillet, make sure it will fit inside of your jar.
- ☐ Fill the jar with your sliced fish and pack it tightly.
- ☐ Add 1 teaspoon of salt in each jar.
- ☐ Pour water on the fish in the canner (about an inch or two).
- ☐ Wipe any spills, seal and tighten the ring around the jars.
- ☐ Add lids and rings to jars, tightening just to finger-tight. No need to wrench the lids on with all your strength.
- ☐ Put your jars into the pressure canner and set on a rack inside the canner.
- ☐ Turn the heat back on and allow the pressure to build-up.
- ☐ Once the steam is pouring out through the valve, set a timer and allow it to continue venting for 10 minutes.
- ☐ Leave the jars to cool for 1 to 2 hours.
- ☐ And your chicken is ready to be stored.

Pork Recipe

- [ ] Get your piece of pork.
- [ ] Wash; remove bones, fats or any gristle.
- [ ] Cut the pork to steaks, fillet or cubes, make sure it will fit inside of your jar.
- [ ] Fill the jar with your sliced pork and pack it tightly.
- [ ] Add 1 teaspoon of salt in each jar.
- [ ] Pour water on the pork in the canner (about an inch or two).
- [ ] Wipe any spills, seal and tighten the ring around the jars.
- [ ] Add lids and rings to jars, tightening just to finger-tight. No need to wrench the lids on with all your strength.
- [ ] Put your jars into the pressure canner and set on a rack inside the canner.
- [ ] Turn the heat back on and allow the pressure to build-up.
- [ ] Once the steam is pouring out through the valve, set a timer and allow it to continue venting for 10 minutes.
- [ ] Leave the jars to cool for 1 to 2 hours.
- [ ] And your pork ready to be stored.

Turkey Recipe

- [ ] Get your turkey.
- [ ] Wash; remove any fats, silver skin, or bones.
- [ ] Cut the turkey into cubes and make sure that the cubes will fit into your jars.
- [ ] Boil or bake to steam the turkey until it is 2/3 done.
- [ ] Fill the jars with the turkey cubes. Add salt if desired.
- [ ] Pour hot boiling water on the turkey in the jars.
- [ ] Wipe any spills, seal and tighten the ring around the jars.
- [ ] Add lids and rings to jars, tightening just to finger-tight. No need to wrench the lids on with all your strength.
- [ ] Put your jars into the pressure canner and set on a rack inside the canner.
- [ ] Turn the heat back on and allow the pressure to build-up.
- [ ] Once the steam is pouring out through the valve, set a timer and allow it to continue venting for 10 minutes.
- [ ] Leave the jars to cool for 1 to 2 hours.
- [ ] And your turkey is ready to be stored.

Notes

Add Your Favorite Recipes

The End

CPSIA information can be obtained
at www.ICGtesting.com
Printed in the USA
LVHW101259150920
666072LV00009B/1072